I0481214

Leadership Development Essentials

Laurence Carter

Leadership Development Essentials

Copyright © 2018 by Laurence Carter

By: Laurence Carter

ISBN-13: 978-1984131492

ISBN-10: 1984131494

Contents   Page Number

Contents   Page Number

Foreword

This text Leadership Development Essentials is written in order to present a conceptual framework for basic training in Leadership Development for individuals who aspire to learn to be leaders. In undertaking this book, the first section of the text is used to outline in the simplest way possible, some of the basic principles of leadership and organisational structure that need to be understood in order to effectively prepare individuals for training so as to develop their leadership abilities and skills.

In part two of this book, a simple framework is used to outline for review basic leadership characteristics and principles that should be learnt and applied by leaders in their leadership efforts. There is no effort on my part to micro manage content so as to push any particular narrative or preference for leadership characteristics or style that should be applied in any and all circumstances.

Instead I have outlined the topic areas that generally have to be addressed in any form of leadership training and it is up to the persons who conduct the training to narrow the focus to the areas that they believe are relevant and necessary to the context in which they are conducting their leadership development training exercise.

Therefore for example, personal integrity is mentioned as a necessary character trait for leaders, but it is then up to the trainer to decide if there should be an intense focus on training a person in this character trait, based on the situational and contextual needs of the environment in which the training is to be completed. In using this approach it is my hope that this book can be used to help effectively train persons in basic leadership development. The text uses some of my notes that I would use as a leadership trainer and I hope that these can now be used by others for leadership training purposes.

Introduction

For persons who desire to be leaders, it is important that they work to attain an understanding of basic leadership development principles. These potential leaders should also embrace the need to undertake the appropriate training that is required, in order to learn the leadership skills that are of critical importance to the development of today's organisational managers and leaders.

The idea behind leadership training and development – with a special emphasis being placed on personal development, is the notion that there is a need to increase the **leadership skills, ability** and **capacity** of those who are in line for leadership roles in organisations.

That overall growth in the leadership capacity of an individual is an important aspect of their leadership development process that they should strive for. We tend to concentrate on developing individual skills, and sometimes forget that we also have to build persons capacity to undertake tasks. The reality is that life is repetitive in nature, and personal leadership abilities need to be used in a repetitive way as a leader, time and time again.

Most organisations that initiate leadership training and development programs concentrate on skill development but to achieve the goal of improving organisational results they also need to find ways to build the capacity of their leaders **to perform consistently and effectively over extended periods of time.**

Leaders have to be able to perform in ever changing environments, and be able to meet the long term challenges that this can pose to their leadership abilities and skills. This means for organisational leaders, that they should be able to achieve a high level of adaptable performance that must be instituted over extended periods of time, such as for example yearly business cycles. To do this then requires leaders to have the capacity to deliver sustained results in ever changing circumstances, and not just to showcase enhanced leadership skills over a short period of time.

Leadership development training will often focus on the development of what have been identified as key leadership skills and abilities. It also focuses efforts on adjusting leader attitudes, personality and character traits, which may be adversely affecting the ability of a leader to be effective in their role. Character trait development holds the key to building leadership capacity, as personality traits like patience and persistence, are necessary in order to build the leadership capacity of any leader.

By extension, this means that the overall long term success of leadership development programs, will often hinge on the level of personal improvement that can be attained by individuals, in terms of the skills, abilities, and character traits of those that are being trained. These characteristics that have been identified will then often influence the continued design and quality of the leadership development program and its associated behavioural support mechanisms that can be used so as to help ensure its success.

The mentoring and leadership support programs that are used by organisations to put into practice what is learned by individuals in leadership training, should be effective enough in their content and context so as to alter the behaviour and skill sets of those that need to be trained and developed over the course of time.

As such, the success of any developmental effort is tied to the abilities of those being developed as much as it is dependent on the quality of the developmental program and its related mentoring and support structures that are being utilized.

Acknowledging the challenge for the need for effective leadership training and subsequent mentoring where you can practice what has been taught, should then help to guide the careful planning and execution of the developmental process for leadership training programs. This then helps to ensure that the correct focus is paid to developing the right learning processes for leaders that will produce the required developmental results that can benefit the individual and the organisation that they serve.

It must also be considered that leadership development training often takes place with an organisational setting where there is a need to align the leadership efforts of its leaders with the prevailing organisational processes, which may be the true cause of perceived leadership ineffectiveness. As such, leaders can only sometimes become as good as what they learn and the context in which they operate. This means that often times what they know how to do and what they can implement is limited by organisational processes and resources that in turn may be hindering their capacity for further leadership development.

There is also the challenge of implementing leadership development training in an organisation, with the focus of this effort being built around succession planning for the departure of current leadership, especially in complex organisations. Often times this form of leadership training requires the individual to be assigned to various organisational departments so that they can gain insights and experience into the operations of the department, so as to supplement the theoretical leadership training program that is being implemented.

This effort to mentor and expose the individual to organisational processes, then becomes the focus of leadership development as you endeavour to create a leader for the future of the organisation. The focus is on familiarizing leaders with the knowledge of how to run the operations of key departments in the organisation, as opposed to concentrating primarily on personal skill and knowledge development of a more narrow focus.

The challenge for leadership trainers in terms of learning design for leadership development training becomes, how best to take all these factors into consideration and use these challenges to create a leadership training program that will work for any specific organisation.

In a case for example in an organisation where basic leadership skills are limited in those persons that are to be trained, a skill development based approach for leadership training may work well. In a case where the individuals to be trained already have many of the prerequisite skill sets required of a leader, there may be a greater need to design a training program that works on developing their vision or transformational techniques or their personal attitudes towards leadership.

So leadership training and its associated developmental programs must be able to reconcile these different challenges and take approaches to training that can help persons adapt to the prevailing circumstances and organisational processes that they face as leaders. This then helps them in the preparation that is required for their roles as leaders.

It also helps leadership trainers to realise that they must identify the common leadership skills, abilities, attitudes and character traits that are needed regardless of the organisational circumstances, and ensure that leaders are fully trained in these areas. We then help potential leaders to build the capacity to lead in their prevailing circumstances, through mentoring programs that are aligned to develop the key attributes that are needed for them to be able to lead in the organisational operating environment that they will face.

In part one of this book, we will examine some of the core concepts that that leaders must appreciate as they work to evolve into competent and successful leaders. These concepts that will be discussed will represent some of the different aspects of the context in which leaders operate that make the development of certain types of leadership abilities and skills in a leader to address these challenges so important.

In part two of this book we will go through a basic leadership training program in a simple form that addresses many common themes and how these themes should be applied to the practice of a leader of their leadership skills in an organisational or group setting. This is done in an effort to illustrate to individuals how to apply in a practical sense, these leadership concepts to the circumstances that they will face as leaders.

Part One

In the first section of this book the basic concepts that are essential to the leadership process will be reviewed in a simple and straightforward way. Some of the principles of leadership and organisational structure will be reviewed. These concepts need to be understood by potential organisational leaders in order to effectively prepare individuals for further training for the purpose of developing their leadership abilities and skills.

Leadership Development Essentials

Becoming a Leader

One of the most common desires of individuals is to be a leader of a group of some form, whether it is a business or some other form organisation or social grouping. They are of course several different types of groups that you may find yourself affiliated with or directly a part of, which then allows you to be a leader in some capacity. Leadership on your part can also be practiced based on the situational circumstances that you can find yourself in.

Whatever the prevailing situation, in order for you to become a leader, it will certainly require that you work to develop the ability to have influence over a group of people or individuals that are gathered together for some purpose. That ability to influence others will be practiced in an environment of either formal or informal structures that make having authority over others possible.

The ability to lead others also can materialize from a common shared spirit, beliefs, values and attitudes that will enable you to lead and influence others in order to encourage them to work towards predetermined outcomes.

It is clear that one can conclude from an examination of many organisations that the spirit of the leader has an effect on the way the organisation operates. This happens in some groupings to the extent that it is one of the first things that is apparent to everyone concerned when interacting with an organisation and its members.

In the overall scheme of things it is not always going to be easy to be a leader. You may be blessed enough to lead a grouping that has simple processes and is easy to manage. It will be even tougher however to lead complex organisations, that have challenging operating processes that are also existing in ever changing external and internal environments. As a leader even if you manage to conquer the challenges of the organisational circumstances that prevail, you still will face the tough challenge of managing the human resources that constitute an organisation.

One of the key things that make leading so difficult at times is the managing of interpersonal relationships that is integral to your ability to lead others. Leading the organisation means being able to lead people. Leading people requires excellent interpersonal skills and even then, sometimes that is not enough because individuals can prove to be very difficult to manage at times.

It can be very satisfying as a leader to be able to surmount the challenges that come with leading individuals in varying circumstances. It can also prove to be very frustrating, especially in relation to finding ways to manage the interpersonal interactions that are an integral part of being an organisational leader.

This struggle with interpersonal relationships happens because of our human preferences as it relates to human interactions that make it difficult for us as individuals to geld together in spirit, attitudes, beliefs and everything else that is required to make relationships work so as to help organisations function effectively.

That is why there is at times, such a dependence on formal structures and authoritative leadership styles to help organisation with this process. These formal and informal organisational structures however can be a double edge sword. They can work in your favour to be able to keep individuals in line with group norms, or it can prove to be a source of conflict as individual's rebel against externally installed forms of authority, and instead try to have things function according to their own individual preferences.

One of the other challenges of being a leader relates to human expectations of what you can and cannot do as a leader. Leaders will find that their followers expend alot of their time examining and judging their every move. Individuals will examine your personal life, and form an opinion on the constitution of your character as a result of this examination.

This high level of personal scrutiny can be too much for some persons, and can make being a leader rather difficult. As a leader you have to learn to endure the personal attacks on your integrity, and character, that accompanies being in leadership roles. This means that you have to learn to accept that your life is open to scrutiny and criticism, and learn to deal with the consequences of this reality.

That level of personal perfection that is expected of a leader rarely exists, but is still expected from leaders by their followers. This makes your task of leading, at times even more trying as you feel compelled to try to work and live up to these high expectations.

That challenge comes as well with leaders who are making the effort to build their personal popularity as a leader, which can in itself lead you to be open to attacks on your personal integrity if you find yourself making compromises in order to build or maintain your popularity with your followers.

That challenge of learning to do what it takes to become a good leader should drive you to learn to find ways to manage your own actions, so that you can lead and manage others, when you have first learned to effectively manage yourself.

To be truly effective as a leader, there are so many variables that have to be taken into consideration, and they are also many skills and disciplines that need to be learned and mastered. Some of these are more critical than others.

They are also many forms of personal and organisational challenges that leaders can and will face. Next we will look at some of these possible individual, situational and institutional challenges that a leader may face and how they can impact on the ability of a leader to be effective in their role.

The Challenges that Leaders Face!

As part of your effort to become a successful leader, it is necessary at times to understand the situational circumstances that exist in the arena where you are going to be a leader from a historical perspective. The reason for this is that you should try to have an understanding of what are the positives and negatives, which have been impacting a group of individuals or an organisation, in the past, that has for all intents and purposes gotten them to the stage they are at today.

It may be that as a leader you will be given the chance to start a new grouping and in doing so you have the freedom to create an organisation that functions in an effective way. However often times, leaders come into organisations that have been in existence for a while, that have their own special set of peculiarities. In light of this fact, the challenge that leaders face is the need to adjust to or make adjustments to an operational structure what has already been in existence before your arrival as a new leader in the organisation.

On examining an organisations history, you may find that the operational dynamics of that institution may have developed many positive or negative values and underlying processes that control the functioning of the grouping. Group or organisational choices, made in the past, may have lead to excellent operational results as articulated by the mission of the institution. This is something that as a leader you would then want to continue to duplicate or improve on, as you work to lead the organisation.

It may also be that your analysis of the organisation points to major operational failures by that entity in achieving its stated objectives. These problems that you identify could be legal, ethical or procedural problems that you would want to work to correct so that the institution can be lead in such a way as to avoid these issues happening again in the future. This knowledge about group or organisational history helps you to effectively set the platform to lead such a grouping going forward.

The reason for reviewing past organisational events is that the context in which the leadership of a group or organisation has developed in the past, will affect how the leadership of its present leader is accepted and directed in the present. In the present how an organisation is being lead, will reflect to some extent what has happened in the past, and as a consequence what has happened in the past will help you as a leader to determine what should happen in the future of the grouping.

This concept of understanding past events that have impacted groups or organisations, is important because it allows you to ascertain what are the values and belief structures that drives the thinking of individuals in the group, and what motivates individuals to come together to be part of the group. All these things are relevant to your long term ability to be able to manage an organisation.

When some leaders conduct organisational reviews they often times may decide to alter the institutions operational processes in order to change things to how they personally prefer to get things done.

It may be that a new approach is needed, but as leaders we must at times also accept that if what is done works for a particular set of individuals and circumstances, even if it is not your preference, it may then be in everyone's best interest to let the process remain as it is rather than force unfamiliar concepts on to people because of your own personal preferences.

While compromise may be necessary at times on the part of individuals to accommodate the preferences of others, we have to be careful as leaders about imposing our personal preferences on groups of individuals or the organisations we lead. Leaders must work to impose best practices that work within organisational settings, which may or may not line up with your personal preferences.

Choices that are made by leaders, which will impact on the future of an organisation or grouping, will often reflect how leaders rationalize the historical continuum of the organisation's life from the past, to the present. Those choices will reflect what the leader perceives the future holds for the organisation and its individual members.

References will no doubt be made to what has happened previously, what is going on in the present, and how the future may unfold – as determinants as to how decisions will be made.

This highlights another major challenge for any leader, as progress over time for any grouping or organisation, requires the ability to change and adapt. By extension this means that a leader has to be able to adjust to a constantly changing environment and be willing to change the way things are done, when it is necessary to do so. This means that leaders should learn to be flexible in their ways and be willing to change and lead others through those changes, when it is necessary to do so.

Adaptability and Driving Change

One of the biggest challenges that any leader can face is the need to be able to bring about change within an organisation and in doing so help adapt the behaviour and those around them to the changing circumstances that the organisation may find itself in.

The leader of any organisation will always be faced with the challenge of having to at some point to manage changes to the way key processes in the institution are completed. Change also reaches into the area of relationships as changes in organisation staff can also force the need for behavioural adjustments to take place within the organisation.

For a leader to be able to drive change requires a willingness on their part to adapt to the new circumstances that they will face and to be willing to lead others into making the adjustments that are necessary to adjust to the new realties that they will face. Adaptability is so very important, but leaders must also acknowledge the challenge of knowing when and what we should and should not adapt in the prevailing circumstances.

Leaders cannot dwell in the past and live on past achievements. It is unfortunate that in many groupings or organisations, leaders do not appreciate that times are changing and they have to move on to new ways of getting tasks completed. But the other side of this is that leaders have to know when not to try to change what does not need to be changed.

Careful evaluation of the prevailing circumstances lets you know when to hold steady in your efforts and processes, and when you need to make changes in order address the prevailing circumstances that the institution may face. The prevailing economic and social environment of today is one that requires the embracing of the need to be willing to make changes at a rapid pace. Any leader, who is not willing to adapt to the reality of our changing circumstances, and have an understanding of how to assist others to cope with change, will find it difficult to lead effectively and successfully. Driving change is an important element of a leader's responsibility.

Managing organisational change requires that a leader be able to communicate effectively, with organisational members to be able to lead them strategically through the many challenges that they are liable to face when trying to implement changes. It requires leaders to have the ability to identify the factors that are triggering resistance to change and be able to address them with individuals as circumstances require.

Leaders should be willing to collaborate and negotiate with others, through the use of effective communication methods so that they can create an atmosphere that allows them to implement the changes that are required in the institution. With this is mind, lets us move on to one of the key challenges that leaders will face which is that of the need for them to be effective communicators.

Communication

Communication from organisational leaders must be geared towards the sharing information through strategic forms of communication that then encourages the achievement of the stated objectives of an organisation. There is a body of communication in any organization that will help you to achieve your stated goals and this communication methodology must be effectively developed for there to be success in your efforts as a leader.

Too often, one of the main failures of leadership is the inability to effectively communicate their vision, objectives and goals to those who they lead. Furthermore leaders have to be able to communicate in a way that is geared to generating results. The communication methods that are used must inspire and motivate individuals to be energized to work to achieve the stated objectives of the grouping.

There is also a tendency for leaders over time, to unfortunately isolate themselves with their interactions to those with whom they are comfortable working with. This hinders them at times, from sometimes being able to communicate effectively with the wider membership of their grouping. It also hinders them from getting the required support that they need from persons who they have isolated themselves from, but from whom they need help in order to succeed with the organisational endeavours.

There needs to be a willingness on the part of the leader to be able to surround themselves with those who they like and trust, and those that they do not like and may not be able to trust – and be able to work and communicate comfortably with both groups.

Leaders need to be willing to communicate to those that they can trust with information and to complete assigned tasks, and those that they may not trust as much, but still need to find a way to work and relate with them. Human nature makes this difficult to do, but it still is a challenge that leaders need to conquer as it is not wise to only surround yourself with 'yes' men and women, who will not challenge you to think and do better.

It is also not wise to only communicate to a choosen few and then expect those from whom you have withdrawn yourself to still willingly follow your directions. It is important for leaders to learn to embrace those who are effective at their work, and that can lend some functionality to a grouping or organisation.

You may not like them personally but their expertise is needed, so you have to learn to work with them for the good of the organisation. The input of some persons that you may not be comfortable with is worth at times, far more than your discomfort with their shortcomings.

Leaders must create an environment that fosters and encourages open, two way communications between themselves and those that they lead. Leaders must learn to embrace those who can contribute, and not only those with whom you are comfortable.

Perseverance

Leaders must have perseverance. Perseverance in a leader is shown when they develop the capacity to identify a goal and consistently work to achieve the stated objective despite all the hurdles that they may face. You have to develop that personal ability to keep fighting on to complete a task, no matter the circumstances and not be prone to easily quit and give up on situations and people.

This perseverance, that leaders should have, comes with two other companions, patience and persistence. Perseverance requires patience. Many leadership activities are repetitious actions that need to be repeated time and time again in order to attain success. This requires patience and persistence so as to be able to do this as a leader, which then leads to you learning to persevere with situations especially when times are difficult.

For leaders perseverance can be a tough challenge to deal with. However please note though that sometimes you do need to stop with some situations, and to disassociate yourself from some people so it really is not only about persistence, but also developing the ability to use good judgment as to when to push ahead with some projects and people, and when at times you need to stop and move on.

As a leader you need to develop that ability to persevere in tough circumstances. The perseverance that you learn helps you to work through situations even when times are tough for a protracted period of time. Such an intense ability to stay focused also necessitates the human quality of determination; determination requires perseverance, and your perseverance with an assigned task gains results.

Determination requires a willingness to sacrifice oneself at times in order to achieve results. We love to talk about how determined we are, but it can be difficult to practice personal determination when faced with extreme challenges. We must however be determined to make the required sacrifices to achieve our objectives.

As leaders we have to persevere in all that we do, and be determined to complete our tasks. We should inspire others to do the same. We must persevere, we must be patient, we must be persistent and finally we must be determined as leaders to succeed. Those character traits all work hand in hand to help a leader to be successful.

Life Long Learning

Leaders must create an environment in the organisations that they manage were people are committed to continuing to learn. For your own personal development and for those whom you lead, there should be a vested interest in pursuing continuous learning. The example must be set by you the leader and you must be committed to lifelong learning.

This process of lifelong learning includes acquiring new knowledge and reviewing existing information for the benefit of everyone. There should also be a dedication to the practical application of what is being learned. This is needed especially for you as leader so that you can learn to lead others and to inspire them to continue to develop personally as well.

The continued personal development and growth of those that you lead must be of paramount importance to your effort to lead others. A leader cannot be so enamoured with achieving their own personal success, that it makes them lead in a vacuum, leaving those who surround them behind in terms of their personal growth. Encourage those around you to learn and grow with you as you progress. It is selfish of you to want it any other way.

Take a vested interest in the personal development of those who work with and for you, as their success and advancement will be your success if you make the effort to assist and encourage them along the way. You have to be willing to apply what you have learned to life situations, the tasks that need to be completed and to your leadership efforts that need to be applied to varying circumstances. To learn to be a leader you should be willing to apply what you have learned and use that knowledge to grow as an individual into your role as leader of a grouping or organisation.

The Importance of Value Systems and Inspiring Others

Leaders must be willing to set up in the organisations that they lead, ethical value systems by which those around them will abide. Foremost in this endeavour is that they themselves must believe in, and be willing to abide by the same value system that they have set up for those in the organisation to adhere to.

These principles and morals that you have articulated need to be applied first and foremost to yourself, before you seek to enforce them on others. Set the example and be a leader by living by the values that you want to see reflected in those that you lead. Do not be branded as a hypocrite by saying one thing and doing another.

Let your words that speak of your values hold true for your own life. It is better to be an example by your actions, of what you want others to aspire to be, than to speak of it, and be hypocritical in not applying those same values to your own life.

Leaders must also be willing to develop the skills of those around them so as to get work done through others. You will always need the help of those around you and time needs to be spent to develop the abilities of those who you lead, so as to help them compliment you in all that you hope to accomplish.

Do not allow them to lag behind in their skill development and personal growth. You should be working with them to bring them to the stage where they can effectively perform their tasks. Help those that you lead to master critical skills so that they can assist you with your assignments. Endeavour to ensure that those who surround you become proficient at various tasks so that excellence can manifest itself through them persistently becoming better at an assigned activity.

Finally, there is a need for leaders to at times learn to be inspirational in the way that they lead an organisation. They will be times when you need to motivate an inspire those around you so as to be able to improve their performance and to grow them as individuals.

Your vision for the organisation needs to manifest itself at times in the inspiration of others. Do not however let your efforts at inspiration make you full of self pride that leads you to be blinded and insensitive as a leader to the emotions and individual needs of individuals. Inspire and motivate others so that they can strive to be successful at their endeavours and the goals of the organisation.

Remember however to remain humble in the face of your successes, and to remind others of the need for humility in the face of all that they will accomplish.

Organisations and Leadership

The development of leadership abilities and skills for potential organisational leaders has to be pursued while keeping in mind the context of the type of organisational structure and operating culture that each body has and the effect that this prevailing set of circumstances can have on the approach to be taken by leaders to be able to effectively lead the institution.

Bearing this in mind we will start to review the basics of organisational structure with a view to giving some context within which leaders should be developed for their leadership roles. Such a view point is necessary because the way organisations are structured in many ways gives the leaders of these entities the ability to be effective at managing group members, and it also establishes an effective operational framework within which individuals can work to be able to complete tasks.

In examining organisational structure, there are many elements that need to be reviewed such as the formal and informal structure of the organisation, the chain of command, and how work is divided and departmentalized. These elements all have an impact on how persons interact with each other and how the organisation goes about completing tasks.

For example, the way that work is departmentalized, governs how tasks are grouped together so as to create functional departments in the organisation. These departments then consist of groups of individuals that interact to complete particular types of jobs. In some cases the departments may be assigned in a way so as to reflect the need to group particular job functions together to be able to complete tasks as required. In some cases the departments that are formed in the organisation, may be a grouping of individuals that is organised to work together, using geographical location as the basis for its formation. Within these departments, there is task specialisation, where individuals have a set of specifically assigned duties. These tasks that are assigned to individuals often reflect their education and skill qualifications and their level or expertise or experience at completing the task that is required.

These departments then need leaders, and these leaders form the basis of the chain of command for the organisation. These managers, or organisational leaders, are responsible for ensuring that tasks are completed, and they assign persons to the tasks required so as to work with these individuals to ensure that the tasks required are completed.

This is all done in a formal and informal organisational structure that governs the decision making that is carried out, in order to manage the organisation. In this overall system, formal and informal rules, govern how leaders interact with organisational members, both with formal – written and defined rules and guidelines as well as informal dictates that help shape the organisation and the way that it functions in order to achieve its objectives.

As it is imperative that an organisation, have some form of formal or informal structure which is used to shape how it is lead and how decisions are made, we will next examine the formal structure of an organisation and its subsequent impact on how the organisation is going to be lead.

The Formal Organisational Structure – An Overview

The formal organisation refers to the structure that is developed to aid the organisation to meet its objectives. Often times the way the organisation is structured is heavily influenced by the mission of the institution and the best perceived structure that can yield the best results for that organization as articulated by that mission statement.

For example the business organizational structure of an information technology research and development firm would be geared to giving its individual research unit teams more autonomy to conduct the research required to create and invent new technological products.

In some ways this would require a more relaxed approach to the use of formal authority systems and instead utilize an organisational structure that encourages risk taking and innovation, with a related leadership style by its leaders that does not stifle innovation and creativity.

Compare the structure of the information technology research firm that I just described, with that of an established food manufacturing firm which for legal and quality compliance reasons, needs more defined organisational structures to ensure quality control and compliance with international ISO standards for manufacturing for all of its production tasks.

In the case of the food manufacturer you can instead expect a more structured approach to leading the organisation that concentrates on quality and cost control, and compliance to food preparation and handling rules and regulations, in order to ensure that the organisation meets its obligations.

Several management concepts have to be taken into consideration by the leadership of any organisation if they are to effectively organise an institution to function in a way that meets its predetermined objectives. Historically in many ways these concepts and the decisions that have been made, have been influenced by organisational theory.

The general understanding that has come from the application of organisational theory is that the organisation's leadership and its management team would conduct an analysis of how individuals and groups would likely behave within specific organizational structures.

The analysis that is conducted would review overall organisational functions, the organisation's performance characteristics and the control mechanisms that are used to complete tasks and use the conclusions of this analysis to design efficient organisational systems to ensure that tasks are completed.

Within the designed organisational structure, the leadership would be installed and it would be their responsibility to ensure that the organisation then functions according to the structure and plans that have been designed for the organisation.

The leadership would work to ensure that this organisational structure and operational framework is the best that can be used to ensure that organisational plans are implemented.

The leadership will conduct analysis in areas such as:

- How best to create work units / departments, and the accompanying leadership functions.
- Developing work processes for command, control, and the coordination of work activities within the organisation.

- Developing procedures for the distribution of tasks within the organisation.
- The establishments of the required job tasks and individual responsibilities, including those of its leadership.

Understand that organisations are created in order to achieve preconceived goals and its leadership structure should be created in a way that propels the organisation to meet those goals. The fulfillment of this goal then guides leadership choices in organisational systems and helps leaders to choose the right people, systems and work flow processes that are needed to manage and control the organisation.

Leaders attempt to form the formal Organisational structure but all organisations also have an **Informal structure.** This reflects the reality that most organisations have an underlying social system which often reflects the realities of the informal part of the organisation, which works along a process oriented / structured and at times technical system that often makes up the formal part of the organisation.

Virtually all organisations have some form of informal organisation that operates in tandem with the formal organisational structure. This informal structure often evolves out of the activities and interactions of employees. It flourishes in the organisation to a large extent, because of companionship and social relationships that are important to individual organisational members.

Bearing all of this in mind regarding all that is understood about the formal and informal structure of an organisation, these entities and their leaders then work to place the right people in the right positions based on what has to be achieved, and the structure of the organisation that has been designed to achieve this purpose.

This should allow the leadership of the organisation to be able to place the right persons in the right positions in order to make the right decisions for the proper functioning of the organisation and to be able to hold persons accountable for those decisions.

In a sense there is no single structure that will work in all organisations. The structure that works in one organisation may not work in another because of differences in strategic goals and what has been agreed on as the best path forward by its leadership to achieve those goals.

In summary, this means then that the leadership of an organisation should work to choose the correct strategies to use in order to meet those goals that have been agreed to by its leadership, and to also choose the right individuals to work to achieve their stated objectives. Because of this leadership approaches and styles will also vary between organisations, and no one particular style of leadership will be universally utilized in all organisations.

However, it should be indicated that when it comes to leadership styles, that leaders should be encouraged to adopt as a basic style, a servant based approach to leadership in order to address the contextual setup of an organisation. In conjunction with this choice of leadership, it will often then be necessary to choose other forms of leadership approaches to be able to ensure that the mandate that has been given to the organisation is fulfilled.

In other words, no matter the organisation, its leaders are there to serve its members and by extension the general public and the organisation's customers. Then subsequently the organisational context may allow all other relevant forms of leadership styles to flourish based on the situational demands of the organisation. Later in this text leadership styles will be discussed. Suffice to say that it is important for leaders to understand what approach is needed to meet the situational dynamics at hand.

Remember in all things that; **who, what, when where, and why** matters. And as a leader you will get this right in terms of how you go about conducting your leadership tasks if you ensure that you properly examine the context in which your leadership activities will evolve.

There is no doubt that leaders are there to serve the organisation and its publics, and that organisational members should be oriented to serve those whom the organisation interact with as well as their leadership.

As a leader you must remember this and do not get into the mindset that as a leader that you are privileged and persons are there only to serve you as a leader. You must work to maintain your humility as a leader and ensure that you work to serve others in the organisation that you lead. More will be said about leadership character later in this text.

All forms of leadership orientations and organisational structures should reflect that analysis of organisational context that then guides how the organisation operates so as to serve some predefined purpose.

Any organisational system that is choosen must serve the organisations public base effectively and this requires a servant oriented approach by leadership and staff even if subsequently other forms of leadership are adopted that are more suited to the organisations mission and prevailing situation.

Any organisational structure that is chosen to be used by that entity requires a complimentary authority system that governs the control structures and systems that ensure accountability within the organisation. This then brings us to our next key topic in terms of setting the context for leadership development in any organisation which is the authority structures and control mechanisms that must be developed within the organisation in order for it to be effective at achieving the mission it has been created to accomplish.

Authority

The concept of authority as it relates to leadership refers to the understanding that when individuals are placed in a leadership position and they give orders, it is expected that the orders that have been given will be obeyed. To help with the coordination of organisational activities that is a part of the mandate of any leader, it is normal for the leader to be part of a chain of command, where each leader is given the required authority to fulfill his or her responsibilities.

Organisational charts are often developed for organisations and these will show these patterns of authority that have been designed for the entity. These organisational charts are often accompanied by detailed job descriptions for the job positions shown, and information about the job descriptions which then help to define the accountability system within the organisation.

These charts that showcase authority structures in an entity help leaders to manage organisational chains of command and their accompanying lines of communication. Furthermore it defines a leader's span of control and the interrelationship between the organisational functions that a leader must be able to manage.

As a general rule, organisations work to ensure that a person should has only one superior to whom he or she reports and is directly responsible. This is not always going to be the case as some organisations have complex reporting relationships that break this rule in order to allow for the most effective operation of the entity.

If employees have more than one superior to report to, they can have several conflicting demands to obey from different superiors, but in situations that require cooperation between work groups, these conflicting demands can be worked out through participative and collaborative interaction between these leaders. Leaders have to be able to work this process out as modern organisations are complex, and leaders have to be able to collaborate with other persons within an organisation, who they may not have direct operational control and authority over.

A prime example of this is the operations of organisations that are heavily technologically oriented. The information technology department and its personnel often has to answer to work requests from several different operational unit heads even though that department in itself would have its own section head that the IT personnel would have to report to.

These conflicting demands for IT personnel work input to meet ongoing operational needs, have to be worked out in a collaborative manner between department heads and the head of the IT department, for the effective functioning of the organisation.

These IT specialists would have their own direct reporting to their IT manager, but because their expertise is needed in different departments, they have to in effect work at times under the authority of operational department heads while still reporting into their direct reporting head – the IT department manager.

Another challenge for leaders in deciding on organisational structure is that they must choose if they will centralise or decentralise their operations. This is especially true for large organisations, who because of geographical considerations, may have to create separate subsidiaries, or divisions and give more autonomy to the leaders of those divisions and create a more decentralized operation as a result.

Some leaders may however decide to continue to centralise decision making in the organisation, so that the core objectives of the organisation can be uniformly implemented across the enterprise. Some leaders may also choose to examine other alternatives like using project teams drawn from several divisions, to carry out various organisational functions.

These team members would then have to report to the different leaders, on the various project teams that they serve, even though they normally have a fixed department manager that they normally report to as outlined by the organisational chart.

Using project teams is a multidisciplinary approach that gets work done, across organisational divisions. The potential advantages of these types of teams, that allow for flexibility and the use of individual competencies across a range of skill sets has to be offset by the potential for conflicts based on loyalty of individuals to different team leaders.

This loyalty can then make collaboration and decision making slow, as persons in the project teams still seek clearance for their work activities from their normal authority base as opposed to the authority set up that comes with the project teams that have been formed.

In all of this, great effort also has to be paid to the workings of the informal organisation, which often coexists alongside the formal organisational structure. The effect of the informal organisation on operational issues, in both positive and negative ways, often grows as individuals interact and bond in the organisation.

These persons will bond together, usually under common thought processes and viewpoints that then produce informal norms of behaviour that work hand in hand with the formal structure of the organisation.

Another factor that has to be taken into consideration is organisational culture and politics. The organisational culture often reflects the viewpoints and perceptions of organisational members as it relates to the organisational leadership and task completion.

This then creates behavioural attitudes and norms, which then permeate throughout the organisation. Organisational culture and politics have an effect on how leaders work to manage the organisation, and often affects leadership styles and the approaches used for communication by the leadership in the organisation.

Culture often works in conjunction with organisational politics. Organisational politics will refer to the types of decisions and compromises that are made in an organisation, due to the different ideological views of various persons or factions within an entity. For the organisation to continue to function effectively, ways often have to be found to manage the relationship between competing political factions in the organisation by its leadership.

An organisation's political power system can affect in a positive or negative way, its structure and by extension how its leadership goes about building the organisation, and guide how decisions are implemented in the organisation.

All these factors have to be taken into consideration as leaders contemplate the most acceptable setup that can be implemented for an organisation. By extension these factors also affect their leadership context in terms of what are the right operational processes, structure and style of leadership that can most effectively work within the context of the realities of the contemplated organisational structure of any institution.

Authority and its effect on the context in which leaders learn their skill sets, cannot be discussed without making reference to delegation, responsibility and accountability. It is important to understand that these concepts all work in parallel with each other and a leader must utilize them correctly when necessary in order to increase their effectiveness as a leader. The first of these skill sets that we will discuss briefly is delegation.

Delegation

The ability to delegate is an important aspect of a leader's skill sets that has to be developed for managing people. Delegation is the act of assigning tasks or work assignments to those who report into the leader. Any leader that is working to direct any organisation is going to at some point need the assistance of others, in task completion, and decision making and as such, they need to learn to delegate those tasks when it is appropriate as they cannot do it all on their own.

Being able to delegate effectively is important for the management of the context in which a leader operates because the willingness of the leader to delegate tasks to others, allows them to be able to concentrate on more critical elements of their role as leader. For delegation to work effectively, the leader also has to be willing to pass on authority to others to complete a specified task.

The need to delegate by a leader also requires the leader to have the ability to practice two other important concepts which are **responsibility** and **accountability**. Responsibility entails an individual accepting that they have an obligation to ensure that the task that has been delegated to them is carried out in an effective and acceptable manner.

This then by extension leads to the other important concept of accountability. Accountability by an individual comes about when they understand that they are accountable to his or her superior for performing the task they have been assigned as agreed too. Often times this accountability comes with agreed standards of performance that can be used to judge whether or not the person has satisfactorily completed the task that has been delegated to them, thereby holding them accountable for their actions. These are all important skill sets that leaders have to personally develop as basic individual competencies.

Finally in closing this section, brief mention will be made concerning the connection between the leadership process and the motivating of staff members so as to maintain their morale. Leadership activity in organisations is often times going to be relationship oriented and as such, leaders will have to develop the ability to motivate those that follow them and maintain their morale, when necessary as they go about completing their mission.

Motivating individuals helps them to work persistently towards obtaining defined goals, and this is necessary in conjunction with the leader working to maintaining group morale, in order for organisations to successfully function and move towards attaining their goals. This topic will be expanded on later in this text, but is highlighted here in closing because it is one of the key functions that leaders have to undertake in an organisational setting.

After outlining some of the key influences on the context in which leadership will evolve, we now will move on to more narrowly defining what leadership is and expand on some of these leadership character traits that are necessary for any leader, so as to bolster your understanding of how a leader can develop effectively into their leadership roles.

Leadership

Faced with the reality of the necessity to work towards completing some form of predetermined task, organisations then will find themselves in need of leadership to help to guide them in this effort. This leadership that is required involves the combination of the right organisational processes and individuals that will be then used to achieve these objectives. Indeed for this purpose, leadership can be rationalized as being the ability of a leader to influence a group to toward the achievement of assigned goals.

Such an effort to work towards achieving predetermined goals requires leaders who are capable of setting processes in place to manage the organisation. These leaders also have to be able to set the correct procedures in place to match the context within the organisation will operate. They are also required to choose and lead the right people in that setting to work towards achieving organisational goals.

Be clear however that leadership cannot only be viewed and appreciated in terms of the viewpoint of the leaders themselves. The whole process of leadership is one of mutual dependency and in simple terms, this means that effective leadership requires followers who can work with a leader to ensure the successful completion of assigned tasks.

At times too heavy an emphasis is placed on the leaders themselves, which then divorces us from the reality that their effectiveness is tied to organisational structures and the individuals that they lead in order to get tasks done. While organisations tend to be viewed through the success or failure of their leader, often times these leaders are just a symbol of other systematic successes or failures of organisational structures and processes and the competencies of individuals that make up an organisation.

In speaking of an organisation's leadership we have to consider a leader as anyone who has the power to exercise control over others. Another word that can be used here is the authority to exercise control over others. However examination of some organisational dynamics will reveal that in some circumstances the person with the authority to lead the organization may not have the power to do so.

The power to lead individuals in the organisation may instead reside with another person who may have less authority in the organisational system than what the formal leader has, but instead has the power to lead the organisational members. This power to do so may be by virtue of some form of power base from which the individual has the ability to control the actions of organisational members and organisational processes as well, with little fear of interference from the legitimate leader of the organisation.

It is important to acknowledge at this point that they are many different kinds of leaders in an organisation. Legal parameters require the installment in organisations of **formal leaders** who are appointed according to legal requirements for the creation of public and private enterprises. Furthermore the business or goal orientation of the entity will also precipitate the need for predetermined persons to lead various aspects of an organisation's operations in a formalized structure.

They are also **informal leaders** who exercise influence within an organisational setting. As mentioned previously, they may be persons with assigned authoritative titles, or it may be persons who in the absence of formal organisational authority, still have the ability and power to influence members of an organisation. This power may be for example, seniority in the organisation, or an extensive knowledge base from which organisational members must draw, which then gives the individual the power to lead individuals even in the absence of formal authority to do so.

There will be times that the formal and the informal leader will be the same person. In such a case this may help the organisation successfully move forward to achieving goals by avoiding conflict over issues, between the formal and informal leadership.

This does not mean however that a formal leader cannot successfully lead an organisation in which an informal leader also has considerable power. Once the formal and informal leaders are operating in sync, it is possible to garner the same level of success as if the formal and informal leader is the same person.

The Formal Organisation

A leader generally speaking will perform his leadership role within the confines of some form of organisation, or some other form of broad based constituency through which he can lead others. From a more focused view point, a formal organisation will have at its head, a formal leader.

A formal organisation would be considered a structured entity which has been created with the purpose of meeting some predetermined objectives. These objectives may be business related or be for charitable or non – profit goals or pursuits. This distinction between objectives matters as it will invariably affect the way an organisation is structured and lead in order to successfully fulfill its mandate.

The formal organisation will group its activities into structured working departments, such as production, marketing, research and development, and accounting. This allows for work teams to be developed, that bring together individuals with the required skill sets. It then allows for leaders to be established within these departments who can work with individuals to achieve organisational goals, while reporting to the overall leadership of the enterprise.

This division of work, allows employees to fully contribute to the organisation. This is usually done in a format where individuals will be paid for their services, which then provides some leverage to the leader so that they are able to ensure some level of accountability for services rendered.

They are however, many forms of organisation in existence that are by their nature voluntary service organisations. Individuals in these forms of organization are contributing to the completion of organisational goals, but they are doing so voluntarily. This creates a tougher challenge for leadership, as the voluntary nature of persons associated with the organisation at times lessens the control that can be exercised on individuals in terms of their levels of commitment and accountability, as compared to someone who is being paid to perform a task.

It means that leaders of voluntary service type organisations such as a charity that is served by volunteers face a tougher task to find ways to efficiently run the organisation. They often times have to learn to be effective at collaborating with individuals over whom they do not have full authoritative control, as compared to a more formal organisation, such as a commercial business where persons are being paid to complete a task.

The formal organisation and its structure also define the types of relationships that exist between individual members of the organisation. These relationships may be defined by the job titles and departmental structures that have been allocated in the organisation, and the relationship hierarchy that is detailed in the formal organisational structure.

In a voluntary system, these relationships will also exist but with less dependence on authoritative set ups, and more dependence on the collaborative input from those who are essentially giving of their effort and time to the organisation.

The formal organisational structure establishes rules and procedures to be followed by the leader and the followers in the organisational setting. This often entails the setting of power and authority limits, which then helps with the decision making process in the entity. Those power structures that are established often help influence the choice of leadership styles as leaders try to adapt to the authority system that is in existence within the organisation.

Finally, the formal organisation has structures in place that create channels of communication for the passing of information to make the entity function effectively. These communication methods help manage the decision making process by channeling leadership communication through the appropriate channels so that the right persons can be impacted and influenced by the leadership of an organisation.

This is important, as many of these entities that have to be managed can be quite large and complex, and often times the leader, will not be in a close relationship with the majority of those over whom he or she leads. As such their ability to influence will be driven by the methods of communication and the authority that those instructions carry with the followers.

Therefore it is imperative that an effective system of communication be set up in the organisation for its leaders to utilize, especially for large enterprises, with many geographical locations that may even extend across different global cultures. Leaders must be taught how to communicate effectively across these different cultures and within the legal confines of what is acceptable across the different geographical locations within which the organisation may operate.

Indeed the global nature of many organisations makes it even more difficult at times to navigate the complexities of setting up an effective formal organisational structure. The legal structural requirements, and cultural differences that can affect how you set up an organisation, all have a direct bearing on the effectiveness of leadership and the contextual considerations that will drive the decision making process for leaders.

The Informal Organisation

Organisations tend to have a well developed informal organisation that will by nature come into existence out of the companionship and social relationships that exist between group members. For many organisational members, belonging to this informal grouping is important and gives them a sense of belonging in the organisation as they identify with the informal grouping even if they do or do not readily identify with the formal organisational structure.

It is in this informal setting group members can work together under the informal leaders of the organisation to generate common responses to their efforts at working to achieve organisational goals. This grouping can also generate the opposite effect when the informal grouping and its leadership are working against the formal leadership and the direction that has been chosen by that leadership for the organisation.

They are many other factors that can influence the emergence of informal organisation. These can affect the level of power this grouping has on the organisation's ability to meet its objectives and the ability of the leader to manage the organisation effectively.

Autocratic styles of management, poor internal communication, poorly developed organisational operational processes, and the inability of the organisation's leaders to manage conflict situations, are all factors that can contribute to the growth of the informal organisation.

In the best of circumstances, if the formal leader of the entity is also the informal leader of the organisation, there can be some greater sense of direction and purpose in working towards meeting organisational objectives. Even if the formal and informal leaders are not the same person, but these persons can still work effectively together, the entity still has a great chance of moving forward to meet its specified objectives.

Unfortunately, in some circumstances, the informal organisation and its leadership can prove to be a stumbling block that can undermine the authority and power of the formal leader if the two leaders cannot find a way to work in sync with each other.

The informal organisation can undermine the established processes for operations, communication and control in the organisation. They can also especially work against efforts to implement changes in the organisation and instead form a barrier that maintains the status quo.

At times there is also the potential for conflicts of interest when the leaders role in the formal organisation places them in a questionable position as it relates to their role in the informal organisational structure, if they have taken on such a responsibility in that grouping.

Organisational Culture and Politics

The culture of an organisation plays an integral part in determining how a leader functions in the contextual environment that surrounds the institution that he or she is leading. Organisational culture is a mix of shared values, organisational customs, behavioral choices, and attitudes that control how persons approach the completion of tasks within the organisational setting.

How individual members of an organisation, perceive its culture, can have a profound effect on how the entity responds to the challenges that it faces and how the leader goes about managing and influencing the organisation in its efforts to achieve its objectives. Organisational culture affects the types of communication that leaders use to try to influence the activities of group members. It also establishes leadership practices, and organisational processes that reflect the cultural values that govern the organisation's thinking on how it will approach working to achieve its objectives.

Organisational culture helps to develop in the minds of group members what is considered appropriate and in appropriate behaviour in the organisational context. This gives the institution a unique operating culture or way of getting things done. This operating culture then brings unity of effort and purpose to the entity in the way persons go about completing their assigned tasks.

However that same strong organisational culture can lead to high levels of bureaucracy and resistance to change as persons fight to maintain the prevailing culture of how things are done. Leaders have to be careful that in their efforts at cultivation of organisational culture that they do not create an atmosphere that fights change and makes it difficult for the entity to grow and adjust to changing environments.

Inevitably a successful organisation should be able to adapt its operating culture in response to the operating environment that it finds itself in. This ability to adapt then enables the entity to respond quickly to changing circumstances. It allows the organisation to be able to modify its work processes and alter group member behaviour in order to adapt to the changes that are required by the context that the organisation finds itself in.

An effective leader has to be able to build an organisational culture that is correct in its formulation for the task at hand and has the ability to adapt and to make changes when necessary, in order for the organisation to respond effectively to any challenges that it faces.

Organisational Politics

Organisational politics can be described as the creation of groups within the organisational setting that hold strong views on particular issues. These groups work together to advocate their point of view, to opposing groups and to the leadership of the organisation. This then creates factions and coalitions within the organisation that negotiate and collude with each other, when necessary in order to achieve their stated objectives.

Often times, the politics of organisations is grounded in the view points of prominent individuals in the organisation, who rally persons around their view point, which may at times reflect their own self interest or stake in the issue at hand. The political system that can exist in an organisation can affect how leaders, run the organisation, and how they work to manage what is deemed to be acceptable behaviour in that entity.

Just as with organisational culture it can impact how leaders manage the organisation and the processes they use to run the entities daily affairs. It affects the communication channels that are used to address group members. It can also be a source of internal resistance to change and generate conflict in the operational system as political groups struggle with each other for power.

Leaders must take the culture and politics of an organisation into consideration as they shape their approach to managing the organisation. It also shapes how they structure the inner workings of the grouping and this therefore necessitates the leader being able to fully understand the dynamics that are at play in shaping the organisations culture and political influences that are at work in influencing how the entity functions in its prevailing environment.

Leadership and Power

For a leader, the way that they carry out their mandate is going to be influenced by the source of authority and power from which they operate as a leader. For the formal leader of the organisation, their power often comes from the formal authority of the post that they have been given.

In many organisations, that official title of leader, that grants the individual the authority and power to run the organisation is usually enough of a power base from which they can function so as to enable them to successfully complete their tasks. However in many organisations, especially large and complex entities, it takes much more than the power that comes with a title, to be able to effectively lead such a grouping.

In many institutions, there are individuals who have power and authority to the extent that they can undermine the efforts of the formal leader. In some cases, the very nature of the institution, requires that it's appointed leader, be able to exert even more influence that any title can bring.

As such in these types of circumstances, the leader can find themselves having to depend on other personal leadership qualities such as their charisma and temperament to assist them with their leadership efforts. It can also be the case that in institutions that require high levels of professional or technical expertise, the leader has to rely more on their professional training as the impetus for their leadership efforts as persons tap into their expertise as the organisation's leader.

In some cases individuals may not have the charisma and experience to fully motivate the organisation, and can find themselves depending on the use of other sources of power to help them lead the institution. In the normal scheme of things, this can mean using coercive power, such as threats to punish individuals for non compliance to orders that have been given. These forms of fear tactics are used at times by leaders to control individuals and bring them to a level of obedience to leadership commands.

Leaders can also choose to use incentives such as promotions, bonuses and pay increases, as a means to generate compliance with their directives. Using these forms of incentives is a common choice as an option to garnering support for leadership efforts. The ability to use these types of tools can give a leader a very important power base from which they can operate within the organisation.

Leaders undoubtedly, will at some point of their tenure operate from one or more of these power bases as they work through their leadership efforts, and they must be fully aware of the advantages and disadvantages of using any of these power and authority methods in their leadership efforts.

Leadership Skills and Abilities

The work of a leader revolves around driving an organisation towards achieving predetermined goals. This then means that the leader has to work with organisational members, to influence them to ensure that they commit themselves to working to achieve the goals of the group.

This requires certain essential leadership skills and abilities, which are used in the completion of designated tasks in the organisation that have to be carried out in order to work towards attaining the organisation's objectives.

So before we review some of these essential leadership skills and abilities, we should identify some common essential organisational tasks which require the use of leadership skills in their execution. **Some of these tasks that are necessary in all forms of organisation are as follows:**

- Planning, organising, and exercising control over organisational tasks and activities.
- Helping members of the organisation to clearly understand their role and functions in the organisation.
- Helping members of the organisation in the performance of their roles in the organisational setup.
- The overall leadership efforts that have to be undertaken in working to achieve predetermined organisational goals.

These common enterprise tasks, then give rise to the leadership of the organisation having to ensure that they develop the capacity to utilize a range of skills and abilities that allow them to effectively achieve these tasks.

This then means that the leader should be able to utilize some of the following skills:

- The ability to influence and direct group members to work to achieve organisational goals.
- Teaching and coaching ability.
- Excellent listening and Communication skills.
- The ability to maintain organisational morale and to motivate staff members.
- The ability to indulge in critical thinking and to create a vision and purpose for the organisation.

These key leadership skills are used generally in many organisations by its leaders to help guide and direct organisations as they work to achieve their stated goals. This is achieved through the efforts of leadership and group members working hand in hand towards attaining those predetermined objectives.

Leadership Traits

Leaders will need to have certain forms of leadership traits, which they will use in their efforts to manage and guide an organisation. It is generally believed that these traits can occur in a leader as natural talents, but it is also accepted that the traits to lead may be gained through learning and experience.

They are some general qualities that leaders should have, as leadership traits and if the leader does not have some of these personal characteristics as a natural gift, they may see the need to attempt to learn them. This may be possible for some leaders, but it must be acknowledged that some leadership traits may be difficult to teach for others.

First of all before we discuss some of these leadership traits, we should acknowledge that a leader should have enough knowledge and intelligence about the tasks that are required in the organisation that they intend to lead, that enables them to be able to complete their tasks effectively.

It should not be a case that the group members have a greater knowledge base than the leader to the extent that the leader is unable to effectively lead the group due to a lack of understanding of what the organisation needs to function effectively.

It is true that some leaders will be appointed to organisations with a deficit in operational knowledge of what is done in the organisational setting, but have a wealth of leadership experience. In these cases the leader has to be willing to learn the organisation's operations as quickly as possible so that they can be effective.

However unfortunately while some may argue that anyone with leadership experience can be slotted into a variety of leadership roles, I am of the opinion that this is not always a good idea in some cases. The reality is that some industries are very complex, especially technology based industries such as for example - oil exploration and refinery. In such a case you would not want someone who is unfamiliar with the intricacies of the industry being inserted into leadership roles, where complex technical decisions have to be made on a regular basis as part of leadership responsibilities that require a deep knowledge of industry particulars.

We have to accept at times, that in some industries persons have to be mentored through the operational systems and processes of the organisation, and be prepared over the long term for leadership roles in that environment, due to the complexity of the decision making process in these types of circumstances.

When it comes to leadership traits, personal maturity and self awareness are essential personality traits for a leader. Situations will often occur in your leadership activities that will ultimately showcase if you are personally mature enough to manage your leadership duties. This is especially true as it relates to solving interpersonal conflicts and other forms of organisational personnel challenges.

Leaders need to have high levels of self confidence and the ability to appear self confident in leadership situations, even if they are faced with challenges that they personally know that are going to be difficult to manage. The individuals that you lead are watching your every mood and reaction to situations and if you seem unsure of yourself, it will show and persons can quickly lose confidence in your leadership if this is a common occurrence.

Leadership efforts will often evolve around interpersonal relationships and the building of a community within the organisation that interacts socially in a meaningful way that allows the work of the organisation to be performed. For this reason having excellent social skills, will be essential for a leader. Those social skills will be used to build interpersonal relationships and allow the leader to work with others so that they can effectively contribute to the functioning of the organisation.

The ability to listen and communicate is an essential leadership trait that is required, as this is needed to communicate the organisational goals and vision to the grouping. It is needed to manage interpersonal relationships and to ensure that the organisation runs effectively over the course of its existence, through the effective passing of information by its leader.

These leadership skills and abilities are a necessary part of a leader's makeup, and they often work in tandem with varying types of leadership styles which are used to manage differing leadership circumstances. Some of these personality traits are natural gifts for some leaders, but for some individuals these traits have to be acquired through learning and personal experience.

Leadership Styles

The situational dynamics of an organisation often dictate that the leader use a particular form of leadership style, that is guided by the context of the organisational situation. The leadership style chosen reflects the way a leader behaves, especially in relation to the management of inter-personal relationships within the work group, so that he organisation can work effectively.

Any organisation and by extension its leadership will normally be service oriented, and the entity would be in existence to provide some product or service to the public. For this reason, a servant leadership style in a service based organisational set up should be encouraged to be the basic leadership set up for any organisation. The overall context of the entities mission will further refine leadership style choices, which would embrace as well many of the popularly defined leadership styles.

Three of the main leadership styles that are commonly articulated are the following:

- Autocratic
- Democratic
- Laissez – faire

In an organisation that is set up to be run by Autocratic leadership, it is often common that all power and authority that is exercised in the organisation is centred on the choices made by the leader.

In the absence of efforts to consult or involve group members in decision making, the decisions made by the autocratic leader are often enforced by the use of various forms of rewards or by the use of various forms of punishment.

In autocratic organisations:

- Internal communication in autocratic entities tends to be in one direction from leader to followers.
- Since the leader does not often consult with others before making a decision, decision making can be much quicker than in other forms of organisational set ups.
- The non involvement of organisational members in decision making can affect the morale of group members, and as a result there may be resistance to decisions made by the leader within the organisation.

In an organisation that is set up to be run by **Democratic (participative) leadership**, the leader makes the effort to consider the inputs of group members in the process of making a decision. In this form of organisation, a wider cross section of individuals can become contributors to any final decision that has to be made in the entity.

In many cases, the leadership actually seeks out the input of group members so as to encourage their participation and commitment to decisions and also to be able to improve the quality of decisions, within the organisation. This has its benefits as it can improve organisational morale as persons see themselves as part of the decision making process, and it can therefore increase support for any final decision that has to be made.

The drawback of such an approach is that the involvement of so many persons in the process can slow down decision making. It can lead to the leader making compromises that are not in the best interests of the organisation as they seek to accommodate the viewpoints of others in their decision making. It can also create an environment where persons can avoid being personally accountable for their actions and the decisions being made because of wide ranging involvement of other individuals in the decision making process.

In an organisation that is set up to be run by **Laissez – fare** methods, the leader exercises very little control or influence over group members, and instead lets them make their own decisions as to how best they can achieve their operational objectives. Instead the leader often provides guidance and direction as necessary, while not taking full control of the decision making process.

Such an approach is great for developing individual leadership skills, and decision making ability of group members. However if the persons do not deliver in terms of meeting organisational goals, such a set up hinders the accountability for meeting those goals. Individuals may also make decisions that vary from overall organisational objectives which can then create problems within the entity in terms of it working towards meeting its overall goals.

The leadership styles discussed showcases a potential problem that exists with exercising leadership styles, which is that what is an effective leadership style in one situation may not work in another. Different situations and organisational context require varying leadership approaches and styles, and every leader may not have the skill and ability to adapt to using another style of leadership in order to address the situational context that exists in the organisation.

Effective organisational leadership requires that the leader work to identify and implement the most appropriate style for the circumstances of the situation the organisation finds itself in. The leader may or may not have the ability to adapt to the required style, and if they cannot, then it is still incumbent on them to find a way to adapt the best style that suits the situation so as to do what is best for the organisation.

Leadership Roles

Another important aspect of a leaders functions, relates to the leadership roles that he or she would be expected to perform. While we see the main role of the leader as working to influence group members to work towards achieving organisational roles, it is also important to appreciate that leaders would have other critical functions that they would have to undertake in order to ensure that the organisation meets its objectives.

Some of the additional roles are as follows:

- The leader works to devise the correct organisational structures and strategies to achieve organisational goals.
- The leader works to ensure that group member's works towards meeting group goals by coordinating group member activities.
- The leader establishes operating procedures and policies that help the organisation establish goals for members to work towards completing.
- The leader often will be the spokesperson for the organisation and be the individual that speaks to the organisation's external public for communication related purposes.
- The leader mediates disputes, and is often the source of motivation and morale for group members.

The leader is also expected to be a subject matter expert, and someone who individual members can turn to for relevant advice in relation to what needs to be done to meet organisational goals. In some industries, this fact is of critical importance as the operational procedures of the organisation are quite complex and the leader is expected to be able to contribute to the technical decisions as well as the commercial decisions that need to be made.

Finally the leader is expected to be a role model for group members. The group members would look up to the leader as a source of inspiration and guidance, and the leader must work in his or her role to set the right example, in terms of temperament and attitude towards achieving group objectives, for everyone else to follow.

Team Management

One of the key functions of a leader is the formation of work teams that are developed to complete tasks that enable the organisation to meet its objectives. A team is a group of two or more persons who work together and coordinate their activities in a way that helps the team to accomplish their objectives.

Teams can be assembled into functional groups or organisational departments that are going to be working together in an entity to complete specific tasks or to solve problems. Project teams can also be created to tackle specific issues that require problem solving techniques. Teams can be self managed, or they can be cross functional teams made up of individuals from different work specialties that are joined together in a group to work on a specified task.

Leaders should work to create effective teams by working to create the correct team structure, and by promoting in the team the correct behaviors that would encourage team members to be committed towards working to meet assigned goals. This can be done by ensuring that team members participate in group planning and discussions that help with decision making. This is all in an effort to build consensus and support with individuals so that they are committed to working to meet group objectives.

Leaders have to work with team members to build trust in the work group so that individuals can work with each other. The team has to be formed in a way that ensures that it is flexible and operationally efficient at problem solving. The team also has to have the ability to be responsive to initiatives that drive change so that the organisation can continue to grow and mature as a unit.

Team members should see themselves as part of a team, and the leader should work with team members to encourage them to see themselves as contributing to the team meeting its objectives. Working in this way allows for close relationships to form between members to the point that there becomes a high level of cohesiveness within the team unit.

When the leader works to create a team structure that over time solidifies the team into a cohesive unit, this goes a long way in creating an environment that allows for common expectations of appropriate team norms and behavioral practices. This then increases the effectiveness of team performance under the effective efforts of the leader to guide the group to work to achieve its goals.

Organisations are usually made up of many work units or teams and all leaders have to be proficient in understanding and managing the dynamics of team work to produce effective results. Team work can be challenging and this can lead to dysfunctional conflicts within teams, if appropriate structures are not put in place to manage the group dynamics that can lead to these types of conflicts.

These conflict situations can be personality issues, or cross functional clashes that lead to conflicts in terms of loyalty to competing leadership groups in an organisation, and other forms of issues that can lead to conflict. That is why conflict management is one of the key leadership skills that a leader should have, and this will be discussed next.

Conflict Management

Leaders should have either a natural or learnt ability to manage conflict, because dealing with conflict is a challenge that they will surely face at some point in their tenure as a leader. Conflict will often time be some form of disagreement between two or more organisational members or teams within the entity.

Conflicts can at times be simple matters that can be settled with the right form of mediation, or they can morph into big issues that are driven by highly charged emotional factors that can make the resolution of the conflict difficult, even for the best conflict negotiator. Conflicts can also revolve around differences over factual issues; they can also start due to constructive differences in opinion on the direction of the organisation that need to be settled.

Conflicts can start over destructive arguments, or explosive personal or organisational situations that have been allowed to develop. At times, the conflict can be open for all to see, or can be taking place behind the scenes, but in any event, conflict of any sort which is left unsolved can mushroom into disruptive behaviour that can have long lasting consequences for the over health of the organisation.

In working to address conflict in an organisation some leaders work to ensure that as the first line of defense that the conflict is avoided in the first place. However this will not always be possible as some forms of conflict will be inevitable in any organisation. It is not always necessary to feel that conflict has to be avoided as conflict also has the potential to have a positive influence on an organisation's overall performance when it is used to better evaluate and manage the performance of the grouping.

In this regard, there may be disagreements that if managed well, can support the furthering of organisational goals, but if these differences of opinion are allowed to become dysfunctional in nature, they can then prevent the organisation from achieving its operational goals.

Leaders have to be acutely aware as to some of the common root causes of conflict in an organisation. These include communication difficulties of many types, especially misinterpretations, lapses and misunderstandings of communication between group members. Conflicts also arise from issues with organisational structures, disagreements over group objectives, performance criteria and the use of organisational resources.

However you tend to find that personal differences as it relates to personality, ethics, values systems and training, are often some of the key causes of conflict. Leaders have to find ways to work with individuals to overcome these challenges, by quickly finding out what is the root cause of the conflict and then working with the parties involved to find ways to deal with the conflict and restore the spirit of cooperation that is needed in every organisation.

Leadership and Communication

For a leader the ability to communicate effectively is an important skill set that must be present in their efforts to influence the organisation and its members to meet their goals. Communication is the transmission of information from one person to another in an effective manner that meets the objectives for the transfer of information between the leader and followers in a way that achieves the desired effect that was intended for the communication that was undertaken.

For this reason, then effective communication is achieved when the desired action has taken place. This is important as decisions in the organisation cannot be made and effectively implemented without information being communicated between its leaders and its members and teams that have been tasked to work towards group goals. When decisions are made, they must be communicated to the relevant parties so that they can be implemented, that is what helps to ensure the effectiveness of communication.

Similarly new ideas and suggestions to take the organisation forward should take place within the confines of efforts by the leader and its members to effectively communicate with each other. Lines of communication should be developed by the leader within the organisation that allow for effective two way communication, that allows for persons to talk to each other and to receive feedback so that what is required can be understood and clarified if they are any misunderstandings.

Various communication methods can be used such as face to face conversations, telephone, speeches and communication via video links. Written communication can be used such as letters, memos, email, notes, summaries, agendas, notices, and other types of documents. Written communication is often the main basis of communication within organisations, because it can be recorded for access at a later date and signed off by employees as having being read and understood, for accountability purposes.

We also depend on human interaction, gestures, and body language as forms of communication, and leaders have to be mindful of the intricacies of these communication methods. Leaders have to be aware of some of the barriers to communication that hinder the effectiveness of their efforts.

These barriers include, the manipulation of information by persons, how persons tend to perceive the information that has been communicated to them, too much information for the person to process, language barriers, and the emotional state of individuals when the communication was delivered.

These communication barriers can be overcome by making efforts to check the accuracy of what has been communicated by working to get feedback from the receiver of the message to ensure that your message was understood.

Efforts should also be made to communicate by using words that the intended audience understands and not go about creating difficulties by using complex terminology and jargon that is beyond the comprehension of the intended audience.

We have to work to encourage others to learn to listen without a hasty rush to judgment, which often leads to individuals misinterpreting what is being said. Oftentimes persons are too quick to be ready to respond rather than listen to what is being said. This has to be discouraged.

Efforts should be made to monitor personal emotions that may inhibit communication efforts, and to look for non verbal cues that may affect the communication efforts that you may be undertaking as a leader. Leaders have to work to get this aspect of their leadership efforts correct as a fully functional communication process that delivers the expected results is essential to effective leadership in all organisations.

Leadership and Decision Making

Leaders have to be effective decision makers. As a leader, you will be required to make decisions in various types of operational areas related to tasks that are required to be completed. As a leader you have to develop the ability not only to make decisions but to be able to make them in a way that is as objective as possible.

This form of objectivity requires that as a leader you learn to examine the situation that you face and then you develop a range of options from your evaluation of the information available to make the required choices. This should be done without allowing our personal preferences, whatever they may be, to become a catalyst for removing an option from consideration, which may be in the best interest of the organisation, but at the same time it is not your personal preference.

Leaders have to become proficient at identifying and defining problems so that they can make informed decisions. Problems usually come to a leader's attention, through comparisons to past experiences, which let you know that a problem exists with the present situation. There may also be deviations from performance parameters, problems identified by other people or actions that take place outside of the organisation that indicate that a problem exists that needs the leader's attention.

Leaders must work to ensure that the correct definition of the problem is formulated. This then starts the process of decision making that produces a solution that deals directly with the problem at hand. Leaders must keep their options open, as sometimes, the solution you may see as the obvious one, may not be the best solution for the problem at this time. There are times that new approaches are needed and the leader must recognize when this is perhaps needed.

Some leaders also develop the ability to anticipate issues and put measures in place to address potential problems that may occur in the future. With organisational experience leaders can develop this ability. Leaders should also work to become proficient at developing alternatives, to help aid them in problem solving. These alternatives should then be evaluated, using your past leadership experiences, and the information gathered on the situation to help inform your decision making.

At times leaders will face unfamiliar situations where they cannot rely on past experiences to help them access the alternatives. In these cases leaders must then evaluate the prevailing circumstances an examine each alternative from the viewpoint of how best they may think that the choice can address the situation to be dealt with, given the resources available and the objectives that you are seeking to achieve as a leader.

As a leader you also must accept that no one alternative is likely to provide the ideal solution. Every option you consider will have its disadvantages and its advantages. However you must use the objectives you have in mind, to help you choose the best path forward, and make that choice based on the criteria identified. This is what makes decision making so difficult at times.

The final stage of this decision making process is the organisational efforts to be made at implementing the decisions that have been made. Leaders have to learn to take a vested interested in ensuring that their decisions are implemented as planned, since often times the way implementation occurs for decisions that have been made, this tends to be the main barrier to success of any initiative.

Implementation requires group members to be informed of the leadership decision that has been made so that they know what needs to be done. The leader must also make sure that resources are provided to implement the decision, and that the group members are committed to implementing the decision that has been made.

Leaders must monitor the implementation effort, because if per chance the effort is running into difficulties, then leaders may have to initiate another course of action, so as to ensure that the choice that has been made can be discarded if necessary and another alternative implemented so that the issue that has to be solved can be addressed.

The Management of Change

One of the responsibilities of leaders is to manage change within the organisation. Entities will face changing circumstances in their external or internal environment that will prompt the need for change in operational procedures and direction, and changes in personnel over a period of time. Leaders of these institutions should have the capacity to lead the organisation and its divisions through these changes as necessary.

The process of change will encompass anything which causes the organisation to alter its process of operation so as to adjust to the prevail circumstances or to an evolving situation that they may face in the future. Changes in an organisation's internal and external environments are often the driver of change and are often derived from social changes, such as societal trends or demographic changes, or technological advancements that affect the organisations processes.

Internal organisational changes also drive change, such as altering organisational objectives. New leadership appointments or the departure of leaders from the entity may lead to a change in the way the organisation functions. New leaders may have a different vision or focus for the entity and proceed to implement change in the organisation to carry it in a new direction.

In the external environment, the activities of competitors can drive change. So too can the actions of governments, as political and economic decisions can cause institutions to have to make changes to the way they operate in order to comply with new laws or regulations. Some entities decide to make changes in a proactive way, while some only change in reaction to changing environmental circumstances.

Sometimes this change may be gradual over a long period of time, but at other times, circumstances can force rapid and dramatic change. Then there is change driven by a crisis, which often times requires leaders to make decisions to save a situation or organisation, often times without too much consultation with others as they may be normally inclined to do.

For a leader one of their greatest challenges will be managing change as persons are generally inclined to resist changes in lieu of having things remain as they are. They prefer stability and see no need to make changes if what they are doing already is still working. The fear of what the proposed changes can do for a person's status and tasks often drives them to resist those changes.

People tend to resist changes because if they are unsure of the expected new outcome, or they fear that they will lose something of value to themselves, or that they feel that the change is not beneficial to them or to the entity, they will tend to resist the change. The resistance that these persons give, can be used as an opportunity for the leader to discuss with these persons the issues that are causing the changes and to make a case for the new direction that has to be taken.

Leaders must become adept at finding ways to combat the resistance to change that is taking place in their group members. They must be able to anticipate the fears that individuals have about change, by being able to see the situation from their perspective and being willing to make adjustments to the changes that are being proposed in order to alleviate their concerns.

Key to this process is the leader building trust with group members so that they can have confidence in the changes that are being proposed. There also has to be a willingness to discuss the changes and make compromises to address the concerns of individuals.

In summary, leaders have to be proficient at driving change in the organisation. This requires building trust between themselves and the persons that they lead, and encouraging group members to trust in their leadership as they plan effectively for the changes to be implemented.

The training of individuals so that they are able to implement the proposed changes and the communication of those changes to those who will be impacted by the new direction to be taken, is essential. There must be a spirit of compromise between leaders and group members so that any collaboration that is undertaken to initiate the changes that are necessary can work.

Managing change will always be a challenge for a leader but with hard work and a dedication to meeting the resistance to that change and working with others to make adjustments so as to implement that change, will help make that process more manageable and improve the chances of successful change within the organisation.

Leadership Expectations

A leader has several roles to play and these roles come with performance expectations that set parameters as to what a leader has to be capable of doing. The leader may not have the skill sets for all of these expectations, but in areas where they may struggle, they may have to use the services of others that are competent in these areas or work hard to learn these skill sets for themselves.

Below is a list of some of the key leadership expectations for any organisational leader:

- The leader should be able to lead by example.
- The leader should be committed to finding ways to continuously improve the organisation and its functioning.
- The leader should be an excellent planner.
- The leader should be committed to developing a learning organisation that embraces the training and development of group members.
- The leader should be an effective communicator using common communication tools.
- The leader should be able to raise the morale of the organisation and motivate members when necessary.
- The leader should be committed to maintaining high organisational ethics and standards.
- The leader should be a good time manager.
- The leader should be good at building interpersonal relationships.
- The leader should be good at conflict management.
- The leader should be accountable and be willing to maintain their integrity through good ethical practices.

A good leader must be able to maintain their focus on working to ensure that the organisations operational needs are met. This requires that the leader works with group members to ensure that the organisation meets its objectives and that a high standard of operational excellence is maintained in the organisation.

These leadership expectations should be reviewed in detail by leaders. In areas where they see that there is a personal skill shortfall they should make efforts to improve through training and mentoring experiences. In cases where this may be difficult, this is where leaders have to learn to utilize the help of others, who are proficient in these areas so that they can work to assist you as a leader to ensure that these expectations are met in the organisation.

Motivation and Morale

One of the important roles of a leader is that of motivating the organisation and its members. This task includes using various motivational techniques to help encourage group members, and working with individuals to ensure that group morale is kept as high as possible.

To effectively motivate persons, a leader has to find ways to work to encourage them so that there is high intensity of effort and persistence in their individual work efforts to strive towards achieving their goals. A leader needs to understand the behaviour of people and how they can use motivational techniques in persuading them to act in ways that are beneficial to an organisation.

The challenge leaders' face is to find ways to motivate a group of individuals with many different personalities, and value systems in a way that helps them to begin working together to achieve a common goal. The leader must communicate to the group what the organisations common goals are, and find ways to set achievable expectations, including areas of individual accountability and then find ways to motivate persons to achieve those goals.

Leaders should also work to find ways to energize the organisation to work to achieve its objectives. They may choose to use motivational speeches, or other forms of incentives to achieve this objective. Motivational factors differ amongst individuals, and the leader has to be aware of what tools they can use to drive persons to give of their best.

Some common motivational factors are monetary rewards, chances for promotions, personal recognition using award schemes, using competitions and other forms of award schemes such as contests.

These efforts to motivate individuals in the organisational setting require a focused effort by the leader that generates high team energy and confidence and challenges the team to do better and work towards meeting their goals.

The leader can also work to maintain high morale in the organisation. High morale reflects a confidence that group members have in the organisation, its leadership and each other, and can often be achieved without necessarily using motivational techniques.

High morale in an organisation is often a reflection of the character of the organisation's leadership and the trust that members have in the leadership and the direction that the organisation is taking. This results in high levels of confidence in the organisations leadership without the leaders having to resort to the use of other forms of motivational techniques.

High organisational morale encourages individuals into making the effort to give of their best without these persons necessarily feeling obligated to do so based on the use of various forms of motivational techniques.

It is good to have high organisational morale, but be mindful that group morale can be high while persons are still not motivated to work to achieve organisational goals. The reverse is also possible, where persons are highly motivated to perform but there is still low morale in the organisation.

Some individuals place high value on motivational factors, such as attaining bonuses, and some place high value on the leadership character traits which lead to high morale, which is why leaders should be proficient at managing both motivational and morale factors in an organisation.

Time Management

Organisations can be complex entities that require much time and effort to run. As such, leaders have to develop good time management skills to help assist them in being proficient at their tasks. Leaders need to be able to manage time well in order to be more efficient, so that the best use is made of their available time.

To be efficient at time management, leaders have to learn to prioritize their plans, plan out their tasks and stick to the time lines and plans that they make. For a leader, having great organisation and planning skills, is essential to great time management. Leaders must be proficient at prioritizing tasks and scheduling tasks in an effective manner that best uses time to the leaders' advantage.

Oftentimes, it is issues such as poor planning and organisation, too many distractions, and procrastination that are a big hindrance to effective time management on the part of the leader. Leaders also have to be willing to delegate tasks to others and give them the authority to complete those tasks. This often then frees time for the leader to complete other tasks and this helps with the time management efforts of the leader.

Leaders also spend substantial time in meetings, and they must learn to control these activities. Meetings are key time wasters when they are not properly managed, or if they are too many unnecessary and lengthy meetings which the leader must attend. Leaders must find ways to make meetings productive and effective so that they can properly manage their time.

Time management is important for the leader, and the leader must make the effort to effectively manage their time so that they can be proficient at their leadership efforts.

Coaching

Being effective in your leadership efforts involves developing the ability to coach individuals into being excellent team members and help them to become individuals that can contribute to the development of the organisation and the entity meeting its objectives.

Leaders have to take time to find out what is important to each team member and learn what motivates them. Leaders should use this information, to work with individuals to help drive them towards producing exceptional results. Coaching involves setting goals for individuals to achieve, and then through individual coaching the leader finds ways to help show individuals how they can go about achieving those goals.

Leaders should set themselves up as good role models, and set themselves as the example for their followers to aim for. Leaders must be willing to develop their group members and show them the correct way to do things. While working to develop individuals, the leader should take responsibility for identifying individuals that need additional help with their tasks and be determined to work towards improving the skill sets of these individuals.

The leader should ensure that all the necessary operational skills are taught to group members and that they understand their tasks completely and the goals that they should work to attain. When team members then deviate in performance from what they have been taught, then this sets up the need for coaching interventions where the leader can sit with the group member and try to coach them through the difficulties that they may be facing.

In these settings leaders should sit with group members and provide feedback on performance, and then work to provide information and guidance as to how individuals can work to successfully complete their tasks. Any performance gaps that are identified in this conversation should be addressed immediately so that improvements can be made to the group member's performance.

As a leader your task in coaching is to build on what group members have learned in training and work with them to further develop their skill sets. As a leader you must be committed to working with individuals to maintain high standards so that individuals can work to achieve consistently high results.

Individuals must be shown the benefit of working to improve their skills sets as they work to complete their tasks. As they work to achieve their objectives, leaders should communicate with individuals and review their performance so as to help keep them on track with meeting their targets as to their behaviour and task accomplishments.

Building individuals up to live out to their full potential is important and leaders must be committed to coaching individuals to work to meet these objectives.

It is important that leaders commit themselves to learning to utilize all of these character traits, and leadership skills and abilities and apply these principles to their leadership efforts. It will take time to learn these principles, but leaders must persist in their efforts to do so and they will eventually be rewarded over time by improvements in their leadership skills and abilities.

Part 2

In part two of this book, a simple framework is used to outline for review in a training environment, basic leadership characteristics and principles that should be learnt and applied by leaders in their leadership efforts.

In this section we will review the topic areas that generally have to be addressed in any form of leadership training and it is up to the persons who conduct the training to narrow the focus to the areas that they believe are relevant to the context in which they are conducting their leadership development training exercise.

In using this section of the book for basic leadership training, I urge you to encourage participants to read through section one of this text, as initial preparation for their leadership training program. Section one gives the background information necessary to help review the content of section two for leadership training purposes.

Leadership Training Program

Introduction

Leadership Training

For those who have been called to be leaders, the challenge that they face is to embark on a process of learning that matures them into the leadership roles that they feel that they have been called to embrace. To learn to effectively lead individuals and organisations, will take time, as there are many lessons that need to be appreciated as you embark on the process of developing your leadership skills and abilities.

For many individuals, this will be a life long journey of learning, practicing and adapting their leadership styles and processes when necessary in order to meet the demands of the situational context, that the organisation or body that you are leading will face.

As a leader you must be willing to adapt as you will find over time that different contextual circumstances will at times require adjustments to your approach to leadership. As a leader you must be willing to learn all of the required leadership concepts and then use these principles in conjunction with your leadership skills and abilities, to then put what you have learnt into practice in your leadership efforts.

Indeed because leaders are all given unique skills and abilities, your journey in developing as a leader will in a way be individual in its experience, while still learning some general principles that will apply in many common leadership contexts that you will face.

The principles that you learn should be applied to leadership development not only in the organisation that you function in but in all aspects of your life. The reason for this is that you should practice maintaining the integrity of your leadership values in both your public and private life so that your integrity cannot become in danger of being challenged by those that you lead.

In this training we will examine basic leadership principles, and how these concepts can be applied to your leadership roles. We will also review many of the common challenges that leaders will face and use our analysis of these situations to help you to learn to evolve into the type of leader that you have the potential to become.

Leadership Context

As you develop as a leader, an individual has to fully understand the context within which such leadership activity exists. There are a wide range of situational circumstances that can have an effect of what is your mission as a leader. This in turn will help to determine the choices that you will make as to leadership styles, and operational process choices for your leadership efforts and for the structure of the organisation that you will lead.

To examine leadership we must accept certain basic concepts that mandate how leadership should unfold in different circumstances. These concepts form the foundation of the organisation's functioning and mandate how you evaluate what will be necessary for you to do as a leader to be able to successfully lead the organisation within the context of the organisation that you are going to lead.

First of all your leadership skills should be developed in an environment where you remain aware that your primary focus is to foremost serve the needs of the organisation and its members and by extension the public that it serves. Therefore as a basic tenet of your leadership efforts you have to be determined serve others as the foundational basis for taking the entity forward successfully as a leader. Your basic leadership efforts should be directed towards serving the needs of the organisation.

Leaders should also apply some analysis to the organisation so that they can understand the context of the organisational leadership situation. The various factors that come out of their analysis of that context then act as the basis for choosing leadership behaviour, styles and organisational structure and processes which might then serve your leadership efforts most effectively. For enterprise leadership, your leadership style is often guided by the actual organisational situation which provides the context that drives your leadership efforts and decision making processes.

You must learn to analyze the enterprise situation so as to draw conclusions as to the best leadership styles and behavioral choices that will be required for the situation at hand. That analysis will include some of the following:

- Organisation vision and tasks to be completed.
- The nature of the followers that are needed to complete the mission of the organisation.
- The talents and abilities of organisation members that help shape enterprise context.
- The organisational structure of the institution.
- The relationships and events that impact organisational context.

The organisation and its leaders have choices to make about leadership styles. A leader can decide on the one hand to use their natural or preferred style of leadership in every situation, or decide to use different leadership styles to address varying situational contexts.

The level of education, job experience and personal maturity of organisational members would often influence leadership styles choices. For example, persons that are minimally qualified and that lack job experience, and persons that need further enhancement of their abilities and skills may need to be lead in an autocratic way so as to be guided in a more direct manner in what they have to do.

Persons that are well qualified and have the required job experience can then be lead in the organisation by a more participative style of leadership. Their job experience and maturity, allows the leader to give them the opportunity to contribute to the decision making process of the organisation.

How does Leadership in the Organisation Work?

To understand how leadership will work in the organisation, we should examine the relationship between the leader and those who follow the leader. The context and circumstances of these relationships make up the substance of leadership activity in the organisation.

This relational dynamic, also influences individual styles of leadership for leaders as they work to respond to the leadership dynamic that they face in the organisation. This relationship is also influence by organisational structures and processes that serve to guide how leaders and individuals respond to the situations that they face within the organisational context.

Leadership activity may then materialize in the practice of various styles of leadership that reflect different personality and situational demands that are influencing these choices. The style of leadership that is utilized by a leader will often vary depending upon the individual leader and the situation in which leadership is exercised.

Leaders may have the capacity to exercise different styles of leadership in different situations, while some may not have the ability to do so. Their leadership style will give us some insight as to how a leader operates but not necessarily who he or she is in character. However the leader's character traits are often borne out in the decisions that they make in the enterprise, and persons will eventually draw their own conclusions concerning a leader's character based on the choices that the leader makes in their role.

Oftentimes the skill that will matter most for a leader is going to be their ability to get along with people. As leadership of others revolves around relational factors, this ability to effectively relate to individuals is of vital importance.

Leadership style, by definition, is the way a leader carries out their functions and how they are perceived by those they attempt to lead. Human perception of leadership styles often depends on several factors.

The personality and character of the leader, the character or needs of the group to be lead, and the contextual situation concerns, all play a part in the leadership dynamic that plays out in the organisation and how persons perceive a leaders' style of running an organisation.

Therefore it is imperative that the leader recognize their character and personality traits, as well as their natural gifts and talents. Leaders also have to gain some insight into the needs of the people that they serve, and the dynamics of the situation they are called to manage. Doing this them helps them in their decision making process as an organisational leader.

They are many different leadership styles that can be used by leaders to run an organisation. **The most common leadership styles that have been identified by management theorists that are commonly used today are:**

- Autocratic - the leader decides and implements what he/she wants.
- Democratic - the leader involves the followers in both the discussion of the situational circumstances and the decisions to be taken.
- Laissez – fare – the leader exercises very little control or influence over group members.
- Persuasive – the leader sells his/her ideas to their followers.
- Consultative/participative – the leader discusses issues with their followers before reaching his/her decision.

Autocratic – if a leader is perceived as being autocratic, it is usually a case were all authority is centred on the leader. Decisions are often enforced by the use of rewards and fear of punishment. These types of leaders tend to communicate only to their followers and do not often open communication channels for the reverse form of communication to occur.

Autocratic leadership has its advantages as it often allows for fast decision making. Followers may however have issues with morale due to their non inclusion in the decision making process. This can often result in the followers not supporting the decisions made by the leader if these decisions are at odds with their own desires or beliefs.

Democratic – if a leader is perceived as being democratic, the leader takes into consideration the suggestions of group members as well as the leader in implementing decision making processes. The leader considers all members of the group as important contributors in the decision making process.

Taking this approach to leadership often increases morale and final support for decisions, but it can lead to slow decision making, and operational compromises that are made by the leader as efforts are made to please everyone.

Laissez – fare – if a leader is perceived as being laissez – fare, the leader exercises little control or influence over their followers. A member is given a goal and left to decide how best to achieve it while the leader offers advice and direction when it is necessary to do so. While this often allows for individual development of group members, the lack of definitive direction and decision making control by the leader can hinder the organisation from reaching organisational goals.

Persuasive – if a leader is perceived as being persuasive the leader sells their ideas to their followers so as to get them to agree to the required course of action. For decisions that are popular with the group the followers this can be an effective leadership method but for unpopular decisions it can lead to problems if the leader cannot convince the followers of their choosen pathway for the organisation.

Consultative / Participative – if a leader is perceived as being participative the leader consults with the followers in the decision making process. Even though consultation may take place, the final decision is made by the leader. In this form of leadership style followers may still be unsatisfied with this approach as the leader still is the person who makes the final decision.

Leaders may have to change their leadership styles at different times in an organisation, in order to address situational dynamics. In such a case, a particular form of leadership style may be used to lead in situations where it seems to be the right style for the task at hand and the needs of the moment.

The mature leader may be able to exercise multiple leadership styles according to the situation to be addressed. This will not however, be possible for all leaders. Leaders must be aware of this and know when to explore other options to be used in order to address situations that they are not equipped to handle.

Finding Your Leadership Style

They are several other leadership styles that can be used as have been identified by management theory. The goal in evaluating the use of these leadership styles is for you to identify what you believe is your predominant leadership style(s) and see where you may be able to learn other leadership approaches which can then be used for varying circumstances.

They are several manifestations of the leadership styles that can exist in the organisation. **Here are a few more leadership styles which we can examine in the context of organisational leadership.**

- **Motivational leader** – these leaders know how to motivate their followers when it is needed. They know how to encourage individuals to strive to do better so as to increase morale within the group and to improve individual and group performance**.**
- **Team-building leader** – the team leader has the ability to develop effective teams. These organisational groups are created by ensuring that the correct skill sets and character traits are in the individuals who populate these groups in order to get the required results.
- **Visionary leader** – these types of leaders have a clear vision as to the direction the organisation should take, in the prevailing circumstances. They have the vision to pursue the long term development of an organisation and know how to work to get everyone on board with their vision for the future of the enterprise.
- **Strategic leader** – these leaders have the ability to translate organisation vision into operational strategies that can be used by the organisation so that the enterprise can achieve

its mission. A strategic leader is able to get the various organisation departments of an entity working together and focused on achieving organisational goals.

These are just some of the other leadership styles that can be used in organisational settings. Here is the challenge with all of these leadership styles – **when is it appropriate to utilize any of the previously mentioned leadership styles?** The answer to this lies in understanding that first and foremost you must examine the prevailing organisational circumstances so that you can make a decision that points you to the right choice.

Therefore while your preference or situational dictates may point you to a particular style of leadership as being necessary or relevant to a particular set of circumstances, it may be necessary to choose a different path based on the prevailing circumstances of the organisational context.

While some leaders may have the capacity to adopt multiple leadership styles, if this is not the case do not spend time trying to mimic someone else's style. Do what you have the talent to do as a leader and instead draw on the skills of someone else who is more capable of addressing the situation if you do not have the skill set to do so.

Each type of leadership style has its own advantages and disadvantages that affect whether a particular leadership style should be exercised. Leadership styles are options where quite often the situation determines which style is best suited to be used at that time. This means that context is an important aspect of organisational leadership. Leadership takes into account the organisational context in which leadership is exercised.

Every organisational context is unique in its mission, interpersonal relationships, and organisational culture. This unique context is what shapes the organisation's ideology, attitudes, and values that guide organisational and individual personal behaviour.

These same factors help individual leaders to then work to organize what the organisation thinks, feels, and does and by extension it then affects how the leader goes about leading that organisational group.

Leadership has to be viewed outside of the personality traits of the leader, such as self confidence and personal drive, and should also reflect the relationship between the leader and those being led. **They are also some important factors that affect this relationship such as:**

- The character of the leader – **trustworthiness.**
- The leader's **integrity.**
- The leader's **skills and abilities.**
- The leader's **ethics and value systems.**

These factors are relational in nature and reflect the interaction of the leader and their followers, the relationship between them, and the impact that they have on one another. This means that we must pay attention to the character of the leaders and those being led.

This is because for organisational leaders, personal character and how these character traits are used in the organisational setting, is an important aspect of how a leader successfully works to lead an organisation.

Leadership Qualities and Skills

In the pursuit of your own personal development as a leader, some attention has to be paid to some essential leadership qualities and skills that should be developed. Of course depending on your organisation they may be some peculiar qualities and skills that are necessary as it relates to your own leadership requirements.

What is listed below are some of the general requirements that are often common to basic leadership functions.

Leadership should have some basic qualities such as:

- Leaders should be strong in their vision for their organisation and should commit themselves to realizing these goals.
- Leaders help the organisational members learn and should learn together with their organisational members.
- Leaders must have the ability to communicate effectively and be capable of working to reconcile differences between competing convictions in the organisation.

There are skills that leaders can learn through training. There are also some other natural talents and learned skills that are necessary for every leader. Character however is related more so to who the person is, whereas the competencies listed below tend to be skills that can be learned by leaders.

These leadership skills include:

- Listening and encouraging skills
- Communication skills
- Accountability
- Managing Change
- Conflict management

- Motivational techniques
- Problem solving techniques

The challenge for a leader is that they need to help build the relationship between themselves and those that follow them. This involves using many of these same skills and abilities in order to build that relationship. **This also means encouraging in their organisational followers:**

- A strong commitment to the organisation's purpose and mission.
- Open communication within the organisation and between the organisation and its leaders.
- Cultivating a culture in the organisational grouping that takes responsibility for its problems.
- Developing the ability to reconcile conflicts.

Please note:

Different circumstances dictate different leadership emphases and strategies. The effective leader constantly then works to adapt to new challenges and opportunities. The same person is not equally effective in all situations.

Some leaders are successful in one setting and not successful in the next. All leaders need to recognize that point and develop strategies to address areas where they may struggle rather than pursuing at times what they are not capable of doing.

Leadership is a reciprocal relationship between leaders and those that they lead. Leaders then tend to act in certain ways, cultivate certain habits and develop certain types of character strengths, which reflect that relationship.

Effective leaders are:

- Ethical in character and behaviour.
- Have leadership skills and abilities.
- Can manage conflict situations.
- Maintain integrity and respect from others.
- Can bring people together and build consensus.
- Is trustworthy and accountable.
- Can understand and manage change.
- Leader is Humble.
- Able to function effectively in a variety of organisational relationships.
- Listen carefully and communicate effectively.
- Can utilize the talents of others.

Leaders must be able to develop these skills and character attributes in their efforts at personal development. As mentioned previously some of these characteristics may come naturally, but some of these attributes can be learned. Leaders must make the effort to incorporate these abilities and character skills into their behaviour as an organisational leader.

The Common Challenges for all Leaders

Effective leadership in the organisation is often going to be based on a commitment to integrity, and teamwork amongst team members in order to make the organization work effectively. The glue that holds individuals together is the leader who works to unify individuals and then this allows the team work within the group that is expected to materialize.

Integrity is also necessary to the effective functioning of organisation leadership. Integrity is a strict adherence to moral or ethical codes. This is needed by leaders, and this often means that as leaders, you need to avoid even the appearance of improper behaviour so that those that follow you can trust you completely.

Teamwork is a cooperative effort by the members of a group or team to achieve a common goal. Leaders need to be able to work together as a team to achieve their stated organisational goals. The functioning of any organisation often reflects the efforts of their leaders at getting individuals to work together as a team.

As a leader you need to be willing to maintain **high standards**. Standards are a degree or high level of requirement that persons should work to attain. High levels of moral conduct and operational standards have to be maintained by leaders for themselves and the organisation that they serve. The communication of these high standards enables you to enforce and reinforce high levels of accountability.

You must possess a positive **attitude** as a leader. Leaders set the tone for acceptable and appropriate attitude and behaviour. Your attitude to your responsibilities often influences the attitudes of your followers to their responsibilities. This in turn shapes the direction that the organisation takes. Your attitude to the organisation affects performance.

You must also as a leader, be willing to be a **role model.** In order to be a role model, you must first set a positive example. Your organisational team emulates your leadership, your attitude and work ethic. Being a good role model helps you to set the correct example for your followers.

Leadership integrity is also very critical. Leaders should be committed to maintaining personal integrity, and view this activity as essential in all spheres of their life. You have to be a person with integrity and be prepared to lead by example!

Persistence in completing your tasks is also necessary. Without it, when problems occur you may be easily swept away from following through on your responsibilities. Leaders must be persistent, in their efforts to fulfill the responsibilities of their organisation.

Finally you must be **accountable** as a leader. Being accountable as a leader means that you ensure that you are setting high standards, and then that you are holding yourself and others in your organisation accountable for their actions.

Problems That Cause Leaders to Fail

When you examine the lives of many leaders, if they have failed in their ability to lead, the problems usually stem from organisational performance failures or several common types of moral failings.

When it comes to operational issues and the types of challenges that come from running various types of organisational structures, leaders have to face the reality that they have to work diligently to overcome these types of issues if they are going to succeed as leaders.

This is where leadership training becomes relevant as leaders should strive to work to be prepared for their roles so that they can function effectively in those positions so that they do not fail. In some cases, the organisation may face a crisis that may be more than your training can overcome, and in those circumstances even if you do fail, it will be a learning experience for you from whom you have to pull yourself up and try again.

The longer you lead an organisation, the more likely that you may face these types of crisis situations, or changes to the organisations operating environment that make it very difficult to lead the institution, which brings the spectre of personal and organisational failure closer to being a reality.

So I advise you to keep an open mind in the face of these forms of difficulties and work diligently to overcome these situations. However if failure comes, let it be because the situation is more than the organisation can sustain, and do not let it be the result of lapses in you leadership efforts that then reflect poorly on your personal performance as a leader.

When it comes to the other main reasons for failure as a leader which is linked to moral and ethical failings, this is a problem that leaders have to be warned against as the traps that cause leaders to fall because of moral problems are numerous.

In leading an organisation, a leader quickly discovers that they have access and control to finances and power that if not kept in perspective can lead a leader into moral failings and various forms of corruption. Leaders often fall into these traps such as abusing their power, greed, stealing, money laundering, sexual indiscretions and other forms of corruption that can be part of the reality of leading an organisation.

Greed for example is a moral trap that can lead to the downfall of a leader. Greed sets in when individuals become prone to excesses and needs well beyond what is necessary or desirable. A leader especially has to guard against the onslaught of greed in their leadership role. A leader in his position of authority gains power and this power will give them access to at times considerable wealth.

This gives them the authority and freedom many times to accumulate large amounts of assets, both personally and on the behalf of the organisation that they lead and this can easily lead to greed on their part. This greed can evolve into various forms of corruption as the leaders find themselves getting more caught up in accumulating wealth at any cost.

Small favours and allowances to organisational members, business partners and clients can become, major bribes and excesses within the organisation. A lust for more wealth, more money, and more assets can take over the decision making process of a leader and becomes the driving force of how they think, what their priorities are, and how they react and manage an organisation.

Leaders must guard themselves against the excesses that can lead to greed and corruption. Leaders must admit that the danger exists and place checks and balances in place in the organisation to guard against the imposition of these moral failings. By the same token the leader must constantly examine their own activities, to make sure that they are not personally falling into moral traps that lead them to risk falling into the greed and corruption that can exist in any type of leadership position.

Then there is the issue of the abuse of power by a leader in their leadership roles. Leadership and power go hand in hand. Leading an organisation gives you power over people, power over money and assets and the power to influence situations due to the reach and influence that your organisation may have within the society. The power that comes with leadership also brings the possibility of corruption that can be the end result of allowing that power to destroy your personal morals.

Power and its influence within and outside of an organisation, creates the ability to alter the behaviour of others, whether this is in a positive or negative way. The power that a leader can achieve will evolve through the relationships that can be created over time with individuals. The levels of influence based on the power of relationships, can then lead to high levels of corruption if not properly managed by a leader.

For example, situations such as illegal or immoral sexual relationships and other forms of secretive alliances, corruption and other forms of illegal activity, which when known by others, can lead to the blackmailing of individuals, are examples of abuses of power that can occur within an organisation.

The overriding danger for a leader is that the power that they can wield can very often corrupt them. You have to be ever conscious of this danger as a leader. You should be determined to not allow yourself to fall victim to the lure to abuse the power that has been granted to you. As a leader you have to be determined to guard your integrity so that you do not end up abusing the power that you have as a leader.

Finally there is the challenge of falling to sexual indiscretions, which leaders also have to face. A leader is a visible symbol of control and power in an organisation. Individuals love and admire persons that have control and power. Some of that admiration can translate into a secret longing for sexual interaction with someone they see as being very powerful and desirable.

A leader is often made aware of this adoration and they may also find that with the success they have achieved, they may feel they can have whatever is in their reach. This desire can then extend to wanting to have inappropriate sexual relationships with others, to the extent that they can get away with it. Inappropriate sexual liaisons have been the downfall of many leaders and it is not a problem that should be ignored by those in leadership positions.

To protect yourself you have to first acknowledge that it can be an issue and that if you are not careful you can even be subject to sexual entrapment by individuals looking to capitalize on your success and wealth. You have to be determined to avoid the spectre of sexual indiscretions and be determined to stay on the morally correct path that keeps you from falling into these types of moral traps as a leader.

Balance

Being a leader can be a tough and lonely task. It is at times, very time consuming and requires a commitment of substantial portions of your time to the tasks that need to be completed. This demand on your time can have a big effect on your ability to make priorities of other aspects of your personal life.

A leader should find the time to periodically take stock of all that they are doing in both their personal and professional lives. This is in order to make sure that they are maintaining the correct balance between all of their personal and professional related activities so that they can perform at their best in all spheres of their life.

A leader must learn to balance the time spent between their work hours and time allocated to their non – work related activities so that they can find space for other pursuits. Spending 70 hours a week working, will do you no good, if it then causes you to develop an unhealthy lifestyle for what remains of your personal life.

Every aspect of your life needs to have time allocated to it to allow for the proper maintenance and development of each area. This reflects a commitment that should be made to grow and develop as an individual, and not stagnate into a one dimensional form of existence.

Avoid feeling the need to go overboard, with various projects in your life that you feel that they need to be completed, and then find yourself having to back away from completing these projects. This occurs when your schedule gets to be too difficult and the projects too time consuming for anything else.

As a leader there will be times that you have many things to do, but you do not want to get to a stage where you have to constantly drop items from your agenda. It shakes the trust of others in your ability to lead when you have to flip flop on commitments that have been made. That breaks the trust that they have developed in you.

When you start this process of having to retreat from commitments that you have made, it then becomes tough to re-start projects, when you have lost momentum and interest in what was to be done. It also becomes difficult to get others interested in the project again, once you have stepped away from working on it.

When you lead a balanced life, it will help make you a better leader. You will find that you will have a healthier organisation when you as leader practice effective control over all aspects of your life, and pass the same spirit and thinking on to your organisational members.

RESOURCE LIST

Title	Author
Business Studies 3rd Edition	Susan Hammond, Longman Publishers (c) 1994
The Structure of Business	Martin W. Buckley, Longman Publishers (c) 1994
Management	Roger Bennett, Pitman Publishing (c) 1997
Organisational Behaviour 9th Edition	Stephen P. Robbins Prentice Hall Publishers (c) 2001
Managing Change in Organisations 4th Edition	Colin A Carnall, Pearson Education (c) 2003

Resource	Website
Leadership Styles	www.lfhe.ac.uk

www.ingramcontent.com/pod-product-compliance
Lightning Source LLC
Chambersburg PA
CBHW071209220526
45468CB00002B/558